EXPLORING SCIENCE

THE THEORY OF EVOLUTION

A HISTORY OF LIFE ON EARTH

BY DON NARDO

Content Adviser: Jeffrey Schwartz, Ph.D.,
Department of Anthropology and History of Science,
University of Pittsburgh

Science Adviser: Terrence E. Young Jr., M.Ed., M.L.S.,
Jefferson Parish (Louisiana) Public School System

Reading Adviser: Alexa L. Sandmann, Ed.D.,
Professor of Literacy, College and Graduate School
of Education, Health, and Human Services,
Kent State University

Compass Point Books • Minneapolis, Minnesota

Compass Point Books • 151 Good Counsel Drive • P.O. Box 669 • Mankato, MN 56002-0669

 This book was manufactured with paper containing at least 10 percent post-consumer waste.

Photographs ©: Deco/Alamy, cover; Federico Arnao/iStockphoto, 4; Lori Skelton/Shutterstock, 5; Ulf Andersen/Getty Images, 7; Bibliotheque Nationale, Paris, France/Archives Charmet/The Bridgeman Art Library, 8; The Bridgeman Art Library/Getty Images, 9, 31; Hulton Archive/Getty Images, 10, 29; Danil Vitalevich Chepko/Shutterstock, 12; The London Art Archive/Alamy, 13; Wikimedia/public domain, 14; Classic Image/Alamy, 16, 23, 25; Jim Mills/iStockphoto, 17; Sebastien Cote/iStockphoto, 18; Kristian Larsen/iStockphoto, 20; Nancy Nehring/iStockphoto, 21; Lebrecht Music and Arts Photo Library/Alamy, 22; János Németh/Shutterstock, 27; blickwinkel/Alamy, 28; Library of Congress, 30, 36; Bob Ainsworth/iStockphoto, 32; Kilburn/Hulton Archive/Getty Images, 33; Duncan Walker/iStockphoto, 34; Private Collection/Look and Learn/The Bridgeman Art Library, 37; Jarrett Green/iStockphoto, 38; James E. Knopf/Shutterstock, 39; Andreas Reh/iStockphoto, 40; Wildlife GmbH/Alamy, 41; Max Azisov/iStockphoto, 42; Don Emmert/AFP/Getty Images, 44; Photodisc, 45.

Editor: Anthony Wacholtz
Page Production: Bobbie Nuytten
Photo Researcher: Svetlana Zhurkin

Art Director: LuAnn Ascheman-Adams
Creative Director: Joe Ewest
Editorial Director: Nick Healy
Managing Editor: Catherine Neitge

Library of Congress Cataloging-in-Publication Data
Nardo, Don, 1947–
  The theory of evolution : a history of life on Earth / by Don Nardo;
  content adviser, Jeffrey Schwartz; science adviser, Terrence E. Young;
  reading adviser, Alexa Sandmann.
    p. cm.—(Exploring science)
  Includes index.
  ISBN 978-0-7565-4214-6 (library binding)
  1. Evolution (Biology)—History—Juvenile literature.
  2. Darwin, Charles, 1809–1882—Juvenile literature.
  I. Title. II. Series.
  QH367.1.N37 2010
  576.8'209—dc22   2009008786

Visit Compass Point Books on the Internet at www.compasspointbooks.com
or e-mail your request to custserv@compasspointbooks.com

About the Author

In addition to his numerous acclaimed volumes on ancient civilizations, historian Don Nardo has published several studies of modern scientific discoveries and phenomena. He has also written biographies of scientists Charles Darwin and Tycho Brahe. Nardo lives with his wife, Christine, in Massachusetts.

TABLE OF CONTENTS

CHAPTER ONE

Evolution Before Darwin

WHEN SPRING COMES EACH YEAR, "dinosaurs" can be seen walking and flying through backyards across the world. This astonishing statement can now be made because of several recent scientific discoveries.

For a long time, people believed that dinosaurs died out about 65 million years ago. Today the vast majority of scientists think that one small group of dinosaurs survived. These creatures had feathers and scaly feet. They also had long arms with clawed hands, and they stood erect and walked with their feet beneath their bodies. Some of them began climbing trees. This allowed them to swoop down on unsuspecting prey on the ground. Over time they became increasingly successful at dropping onto their prey because their arms underwent

Much of what we know about dinosaurs comes from studying their fossils—rocks and impressions of the bones left behind when they died.

changes. Their arms developed into wings, which allowed them to glide downward. As more time passed, the wings became stronger until the creatures were capable of true flight. They had become birds through a natural process that scientists call evolution.

The theory of evolution is one of the foundations of modern science. It shows that species—various kinds of plants and animals—can change over time. These changes are usually small and difficult to detect, but they add up over many generations, in the way the climbing dinosaurs' feathered

Egrets' long necks, white feathers, and narrow beaks are examples of traits that are shaped by evolution.

arms developed gradually into wings. The final result of such changes can be a new species. Sometimes the new species is more complex than the old one. Therefore, a few more advanced species tend to appear over time. In this way, all living things, including humans, evolved from earlier, simpler life-forms.

THE GREEKS LEAD THE WAY

When someone mentions the term *evolution*, people usually think about English scientist Charles Darwin. In the 1800s, he rocked the world with his theory of evolution. However, Darwin did not invent the idea of evolution. He was merely the first to offer a convincing explanation of how it works.

The ancient Greeks had the first known discussions about some concepts that later became part of evolutionary theory. The discussions took place thousands of years before Darwin was born. Several Greek scientists proposed theories about animals and nature that foreshadowed modern evolutionary theories. One was Anaximander, who lived in the sixth century B.C. He said all life began in the sea. Later on, sea creatures crawled onto dry land. Over time their bodies slowly changed. Anaximander said fish evolved into reptiles, mammals, and even people.

Other Evolutionary Ideas

Some biologists and other scientists disagree that the evolution of new plant and animal species happens slowly over time. They believe the appearance of a new species does not necessarily require hundreds of thousands or millions of years, which scientists called gradualism.

In the 1970s, scientists Stephen Jay Gould and Niles Eldredge proposed the concept of "punctuated equilibrium." This theory states that most species remain stable over long time periods, but then some of them undergo rapid bursts of change. This causes new species to appear relatively suddenly—in only a few generations, rather than thousands of generations.

Stephen Jay Gould (1941–2002) was a paleontologist, an evolutionary biologist, and a historian of science. He taught at Harvard University for 35 years.

However, Anaximander did not explain *how* this evolution of species might have happened. A later Greek, Empedocles, offered an explanation. Some early species, he said, were

weaker than others. They were not as fast, as powerful, or as smart. As a result, the weaker species died out, and the stronger ones survived. This was the earliest version of the principle known as survival of the fittest.

ARGUMENTS ABOUT EARTH'S AGE

Several centuries after Empedocles advanced these ideas, ancient times gave way to the medieval and early modern eras. In those ages, European culture was strongly influenced by Christian teachings. Church leaders discouraged debates about the origins of life. They claimed there was nothing to debate because the Bible explained how

Empedocles (c.490–435 B.C.) believed that there are four universal elements—fire, air, earth, and water.

living things came to be. They believed God created the world, plants, animals, and people in six days. All existing species, they said, had remained unchanged since the creation.

Church leaders also claimed that there had been no time for evolution to occur because Earth was relatively young. An Anglican archbishop named James Ussher set out to prove this in 1650. He examined the Bible in detail and calculated that the creation had taken place in 4004 B.C. This meant that Earth was less than 6,000 years old.

The Creation of the Animals, a painting by Italian artist Tintoretto, depicts the biblical account of the creation.

Later evidence contradicted Ussher's research. As time went on, scientists found many fossils. Some of them appeared to be ancient, and some did not match any living species. Being religious, the scientists tried to fit this evidence into a biblical framework. A few suggested that the creation had taken place much earlier than Ussher had thought, but that some species God had created had later perished in Noah's flood. That seemed to explain the evidence that some species had died out.

However, mounting evidence eventually showed that extinction was a natural process. In 1796 French scientist Georges Cuvier proposed the idea that many species of plants and animals had long ago become extinct. He also thought Earth was many millions of years old. By the early 1800s, almost all scientists accepted these ideas.

James Ussher (1581–1656) used the ancestry of Jesus Christ from the Bible to help determine what he believed was the date of the creation.

EARLY MODERN EVOLUTIONISTS

In the early 1700s, some scientists started talking about evolution again. One was another Frenchman, Pierre de Maupertuis. He pointed out that people often bred new kinds of plants in greenhouses and gardens. That seemed to indicate that some species *could* change under the right conditions.

To explain how such changes might happen, Maupertuis proposed a new idea. He said that inside each living thing are tiny particles from both parents. Later scientists showed that particles similar to the ones Maupertuis described do exist. Called genes, they contain the blueprints for a plant's or animal's physical traits. Maupertuis also said animals can inherit particles from distant ancestors. Over time, he believed, a few of these particles in one generation might disappear or become damaged. That would cause the next generation to undergo small physical changes. Eventually, he said, small changes could add up to big ones.

Another theory of evolution came later in the 1700s from Englishman Erasmus Darwin, Charles Darwin's grandfather. He said species evolve because of changes in their surroundings. Those that could adapt to the changes survived, and those that could not adapt died out.

Erasmus Darwin's ideas about evolution influenced several younger scientists. Among them was France's Jean Baptiste

Lamarck. In 1809 he proposed his own theory of evolution. It was similar in many ways to Erasmus Darwin's theory. He said bodily changes in a living animal could be passed along to its offspring. Over time, Lamarck said, these changes could add up and alter that species' form.

Later scientists showed that Lamarck was wrong. An animal's genes do not change because of what it does while it is alive. His theory was important, however. It

Animals receive their genes from both of their parents. An animal's genes determine its characteristics.

kept scientific discussions of evolution alive. In fact, the young Charles Darwin gave serious thought to Lamarck's concepts.

Lamarck, Erasmus Darwin, Maupertuis, and Empedocles had all been right on one point: evolution was a real process happening in nature. But none of them had provided a strong enough explanation of how that process works. That was to be Charles Darwin's great contribution to science.

DID YOU KNOW?

An example of Lamarck's theory involves the giraffe. Supposedly, early giraffes had shorter necks than giraffes do today. As they constantly stretched their necks to reach leaves growing in trees, the tendency for longer necks passed from one generation to another. Today scientists know that this concept is incorrect.

Along with being a scientist, Erasmus Darwin (1731–1802) was an inventor and a poet.

CHAPTER TWO

Voyage to Nature's Laboratory

SEVERAL KEY CONCEPTS in the modern theory of evolution were introduced by Charles Darwin. He discovered some of the basics of how evolution works in nature. This knowledge did not come to him in a sudden flash of insight. It involved many years of carefully gathering evidence, experimenting, and reasoning.

Darwin collected much of the most important evidence during a sea voyage he took as a young man. This journey took him to remote parts of the world. In these places he observed animals in their natural habitats. He noticed a number of odd physical traits in some of these species. The more he thought about these traits, the more he wanted to understand how they had come about. This led him to what turned out to be his life's work. At the time, he did not foresee that

Because of his contributions to the field, Charles Darwin is called the father of evolution.

his ideas would forever change the way humans viewed themselves and their place in nature.

A PASSION FOR NATURE

It was not by mere chance that Darwin had a strong desire to learn. This outlook came from his childhood experiences. He was born February 12, 1809, in Shrewsbury, in western England. His parents were well-educated. So were his grandparents, including his grandfather, Erasmus Darwin, who had earlier published a book on evolution. They all instilled in him a deep respect for knowledge and learning.

The Darwins were fairly wealthy and could afford to buy young Charles the latest books about science and other subjects. They could also afford to send him to the best schools. At first he focused on medicine, but he found that he had no serious interest in the subject. So, at his father's urging, he began studying to become an Anglican priest.

However, Charles' true passion lay in learning about

DID YOU KNOW?

As a child, Charles Darwin loved nature. He liked to hike through the woods and fields. He became fascinated by birds and their habits. He also collected insects and studied them.

nature and its wonders. When he was a young man, he heard that a large sailing ship, the HMS *Beagle*, was preparing to depart on a sea voyage. Its bold mission was to explore far-

away continents and islands that few Europeans had ever visited. After signing on to do another job, Darwin ended up serving as the ship's natural-ist. (In those days, a natural-ist was someone who studied plants and animals.)

THE OSTRICH MYSTERY

The *Beagle* left England in December 1831. One of its early stops was the then sparsely populated country of Argentina in South America. Darwin closely observed the animals he found there. He took many notes. These filled several journals, and they reveal the wide range of infor-mation he gathered.

The HMS *Beagle* was used for three separate voyages to survey new lands. Darwin was the ship's naturalist during the second voyage.

Among the entries in these journals are those detailing the first of many mysteries the young man encountered on the voyage. In a small region of Argentina, he found two similar but different kinds of rheas, large birds that Darwin thought were ostriches. This seemed odd to him. He believed that God had created all living things, but why would God make two slightly different species of ostriches? And why would he place them both in the same area?

This did not seem logical to Darwin. The two species of birds were forced to compete with each other for food. That made the daily survival of each more difficult. The young man doubted that such an inefficient system could be part of any divine plan. He suspected instead that some powerful natural

While in Argentina, Darwin mistook a rhea (above) for an ostrich. Both are large, flightless birds, but rheas have three toes on each foot, while ostriches only have two. Rheas are commonly found in the grasslands of South America, and ostriches are native to Africa.

force had created this situation, but he had no idea what that force might be.

DARWIN AND THE FINCHES

Darwin encountered other thought-provoking situations later in the voyage. Particularly fascinating to him were the *Beagle*'s explorations of the Galapagos Islands, beginning

The Galapagos Islands are located in the Pacific Ocean about 500 miles (800 kilometers) off South America's western coast.

in September 1835. Few people had visited these remote islands before that time.

Darwin noted that they contained several animal species that existed nowhere else on Earth. There were huge tortoises, bright red crabs, scary-looking lizards, and many unique kinds of birds. Darwin correctly viewed the islands as a giant natural laboratory. He hoped it would teach him something about nature's workings.

The young man was not disappointed. Almost immediately he noticed something odd about the Galapagos birds. Each island in the chain had finches, but they were not the same. Darwin saw that the beaks of the finches on each island were shaped differently from those of finches on the other islands. One kind of finch had a thick beak that allowed it to easily crack open nuts. The finches on a nearby island had beaks suited for catching insects. Other finches had beaks that could scoop up fruit or dig into tree bark.

At first Darwin was amazed and confused by this diversity of bird beaks. Clearly they were all finches. Yet they were all somewhat different. They were also different, he noted, from the finches living on the South American mainland.

In the months that followed, Darwin pondered how such a situation could have come about. He slowly developed a logical explanation. He thought that long ago, no birds existed

on the Galapagos Islands. Over time some finches from the mainland strayed too far out to sea and landed on the islands. The terrain and plants they found there were different from the ones on the mainland. They were forced to adapt to the new conditions. One way they adapted was to develop beak shapes that best allowed them to gather food and survive.

Clearly, Darwin realized, the finches had evolved over time. The remaining question was how it had happened. In the years that followed, answering that question would become the central focus of his life.

The characteristics of finches on the Galapagos Islands vary among species because of evolution.

Tortoise Shells Tell a Tale

Finches were not the only Galapagos creatures that gave Darwin clues about evolution. He also observed giant tortoises and studied tortoise shells from several islands. He saw that each kind of tortoise was physically different from the others. Darwin realized that this was similar to the situation with the Galapagos finches. He reasoned that the tortoises on each island had adapted to local conditions by undergoing small changes. These changes had given them a better chance to survive in their immediate surroundings.

Tortoises and other animals from the Galapagos Islands are still studied today. The Charles Darwin Research Station in Ecuador developed a breeding program for giant tortoises to study their characteristics and to ensure the survival of the species.

CHAPTER THREE

Darwin Formulates His Theory

AFTER RETURNING TO ENGLAND in 1836, Darwin remained busy. He wrote a long account of his adventures and studies on his voyage and published it as *The Journal of Researches into the Geology and Natural History of the Various Countries Visited by H.M.S. "Beagle."* Darwin also read dozens of books written by other scientists about the natural world. He got to know some of these experts and talked with them at length.

All of this activity, which went on for years, was guided by a single purpose. Darwin, a lifelong Lamarckian, wanted to present a comprehensive theory of evolution to both scientists and the public. He took his time, working slowly and carefully. He collected as much evidence as he could to support his views. He fully anticipated what would

At the age of 27, Darwin began writing about his voyage on the HMS *Beagle*.

happen when he finally published the theory. It was bound to cause a lot of controversy, particularly among religious people. He even feared a backlash from his family. So the stronger the case he could make, the better.

In *The Journal of Researches*, Darwin included sketches of fossils he encountered on the voyage. One sketch depicted a *Megatherium*, an ancestor of the modern tree sloth.

SOME ADAPT, OTHERS DO NOT

There was another reason that Darwin took so long to publish the theory. In a way, it was like an extremely complex jigsaw puzzle. At first he did not have all the pieces. Much of the data he had gathered during the voyage showed that evolution was a natural process. Still he struggled to understand the driving force behind this process.

Darwin repeatedly returned to the data he had collected on the voyage. The finches, tortoises, and other creatures living in the Galapagos Islands were thriving. This appeared to be because they had adapted to the conditions on their particular islands. A finch living on an island where the main food source was fruit needed a beak that allowed it to eat fruit. Any finch born on that island that lacked the proper beak would quickly die. Darwin saw that nature tended to weed out finches that were unable to adapt to their environment. At the same time, nature seemed to favor those that *could* adapt.

DID YOU KNOW?

Many people think a theory is an educated guess that is based on little or no evidence. In science, however, a theory is an organized collection of principles and supporting evidence that gives one explanation of how a natural phenomenon occurs.

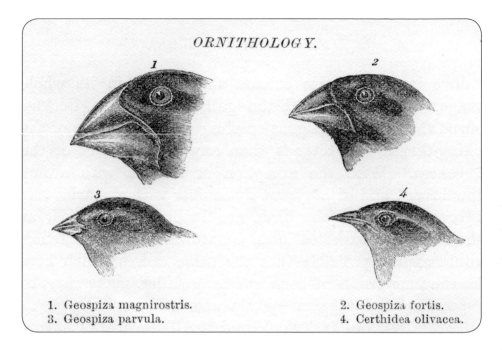

ORNITHOLOGY.

1. Geospiza magnirostris.
3. Geospiza parvula.
2. Geospiza fortis.
4. Certhidea olivacea.

Darwin had to consider the possibility that this might have happened by chance. Perhaps, he reasoned, this process had occurred in only a few random places and times. He was still unsure how it might have worked on a global scale for millions of years.

A STRUGGLE FOR EXISTENCE

Darwin wrestled with this problem until he read a well-known essay about population growth. It was written by an English economist, Thomas Malthus. He said that as human

Darwin illustrated the four beak types of finches he encountered in the Galapagos Islands. He included the illustrations in his book as evidence of adaptation.

populations grow, more people are forced to compete for the limited supply of food. It was therefore a struggle for existence.

It struck Darwin that the situation among plants and animals in nature was similar. He realized that they also were in a struggle for survival. In this contest, all species compete for the same supplies of food, water, and living space. The competition would be toughest, he saw, among individuals of the same species.

In each new generation, Darwin thought, a few of their number would, by chance, be born with some physical advantages. These might be a bigger size, better vision, or keener hearing. Or they might be more intelligent than others of their species. These advantages would make them stronger and more adaptable than the others, so they would thrive and reproduce. Most of their offspring would inherit their physical advantages. Meanwhile, weaker members of the species would be less successful. At times, fewer of their offspring would survive, and their family lines might eventually die out.

More physical changes and competitions would occur in later generations, Darwin reasoned. Each of the changes would be small, but they would add up over time. This slow but steady process would eventually result in a new species. He called nature's choosing of slight variations in species "natural selection." He concluded that this is evolution's underlying, driving force.

A POSSIBLE THREAT

Even after conceiving of natural selection, Darwin continued his research. He wanted to be sure he had enough evidence to counter any critics of his book after it was published. He finally started writing in 1856. At first his progress was slow. Some scientist friends urged him to work faster. They warned him that someone else might make the same discoveries he had made. If that person published before he did, Darwin would lose the right to be known as the creator of the theory.

Darwin soon wished he had listened to this advice. In June

An example of natural selection can be seen with red deer. Males of the herd use their antlers for defense and to compete with other males during mating season (above). Deer with larger antlers have a better chance of warding off predators and passing along their genes by mating.

The Fossil Record

Part of the proof for Darwin's theory lies in the fossil record. The newer the fossil, the less it resembles older ones. This is because evolution causes continual changes in some species. Later generations become less like their distant ancestors.

For example, scientists have found a series of fossils that show nearly the complete evolution of horses. This evidence indicates that the earliest ancestor of the modern horse was a much smaller creature—the *Eohippus*. It was a dog-sized mammal that lived between 60 million and 45 million years ago. Examinations of other fossils reveal that over time, early horses developed longer legs. This allowed them to run faster. Their teeth also became better able to grind the tough plants

that made up their diet. Many other small changes that occurred over thousands of generations made these creatures bigger, stronger, and faster. The end result was the modern horse.

Fossils of *Eohippus Eocene* have been found in Europe, Asia, and North America. The creature is also known as the *Hyracotherium*, which means "hyrax-like beast."

1858, he received a letter from a young English naturalist named Alfred Russel Wallace. He said he had long admired Darwin. He asked the older man to read and comment on an enclosed essay. After reading it, Darwin was quite upset. Wallace, who had no idea what Darwin had been working on, had independently developed an almost identical theory of evolution.

Fortunately for Darwin, he had nothing to fear from Wallace. First, Darwin had discussed his ideas about natural selection with friends years before, so he could prove that he had come up with the idea well before Wallace had. Also, once Wallace realized what had happened, he politely admitted that Darwin had been first.

Darwin had learned his lesson. To avoid any other such incidents, he finished his book as fast as he could. It was completed in March 1859. He had anticipated that it would spark some controversy, but he was unprepared for the enormous impact it made on both science and society.

Alfred Wallace (1823–1913) is also known for identifying the Wallace Line in Indonesia. Animals on one side of the line were native to Australia. Animals on the other side were common in Asia.

CHAPTER FOUR

The Reaction to Darwin's Work

DARWIN'S ORIGINAL TITLE for his book about evolution was *Natural Selection*, but he eventually changed his mind. The final title was *On the Origin of Species by Means of Natural Selection, or the Preservation of Favoured Races in the Struggle for Life*. The title was quite a mouthful, so most people have called it *The Origin of Species* ever since.

After finishing the volume, Darwin met an English publisher, John Murray, who was interested in publishing it. The book was released in November of that year. The reaction—by both scientists and nonscientists—was what the author had expected. Some praised it. Others criticized it. As time went on, it became one of the most important and widely debated books ever written.

ON

THE ORIGIN OF SPECIES

BY MEANS OF NATURAL SELECTION,

OR THE

PRESERVATION OF FAVOURED RACES IN THE STRUGGLE
FOR LIFE.

BY CHARLES DARWIN, M.A.,

FELLOW OF THE ROYAL, GEOLOGICAL, LINNÆAN, ETC., SOCIETIES;
AUTHOR OF 'JOURNAL OF RESEARCHES DURING H. M. S. BEAGLE'S VOYAGE
ROUND THE WORLD.'

LONDON:
JOHN MURRAY, ALBEMARLE STREET.
1859.

The right of Translation is reserved.

Darwin completed *The Origin of Species* in March 1859.

THE WEIGHT OF THE EVIDENCE

Darwin had expected a lot of opposition to some ideas in the book, but he was surprised at how quickly most educated people accepted those ideas. He had said in the book that no false theory could explain so many things so well, and most scientists agreed. Many of them praised the book immediately. By 1870 nearly every leading scientist in the world had accepted Darwin's basic idea that species change over time.

Charles Darwin (right) discussed his theories with fellow scientists Joseph Hooker (1817–1911) and Charles Lyell (1797–1875).

Many nonscientists accepted it as well. Among them were several noted churchmen. The Anglican priest Charles Kingsley, for instance, told a friend, "Darwin is conquering everywhere and rushing in like a flood, by the mere force of truth and fact."

One reason Darwin won over so many people was the weight of the evidence. Some of it appeared in the arguments he had made in the book. New evidence, found after the book's publication, also supported Darwin. For example, he had argued that birds had evolved from early reptiles. Only two years after *Origin*'s release, the fossil remains of an ancient creature were found in Germany. Scientists named it *Archaeopteryx*. It had features of both reptiles and birds.

The *Archaeopteryx* fossil supported Darwin's theory of evolution. *Archaeopteryx* is the earliest known species of bird, living about 150 million years ago.

Clearly it was a transitional form—a form midway between reptiles and birds. In the years that followed, similar discoveries also supported Darwin's theory.

A STINGING ATTACK

Not all of the reactions to Darwin's book were positive. A few scientists, several churchmen, and many ordinary readers rejected some or all of his ideas. They continued to uphold the traditional biblical view of the creation of species.

Some thought that those who agreed with Darwin were hurting both religion and science. Others were personally insulted. To them it was degrading and humiliating to imply that humans had evolved from mere beasts.

In one of the more stinging attacks, a review of *Origin*, scientist Adam Sedgwick wrote: "Species have remained constant for thousands of years.

English geologist Adam Sedgwick (1785–1873) did not agree with Darwin's views on evolution.

No More Shocking Than Gravity

Darwin was a religious man. While writing his book, he realized that some religious people would likely object to his ideas about evolution. He thought that people would be upset over a theory that suggested God did not create all of the species on Earth.

Darwin addressed these people directly in the book's last section. He said:

I see no good reason why the views given in this volume should shock the religious feelings of any one. It is satisfactory ... to remember that the greatest discovery ever made by man, namely, the law of the attraction of gravity [by English scientist Isaac Newton], was also attacked ... "as [being against] religion."

Sir Isaac Newton's ideas on gravity led more people to accept heliocentrism, the idea that the sun—not Earth—is the center of the universe. Religious people at that time believed heliocentrism went against the Bible.

> **DID YOU KNOW?**
>
> Darwin did not directly discuss human evolution in *The Origin of Species*. The evidence he presented dealt strictly with plants and animals. His first exploration of human ancestry was in *The Descent of Man*, published in 1871.

[And even the passing of] millions and billions [of years] would never change them, so long as the [natural] conditions remained constant." He admitted that new species may have appeared from time to time. But if so, God had created them for some purpose. "I can see in all [the natural wonders] around me a design and purpose," Sedgwick wrote.

THE GREAT OXFORD DEBATE

Clashes between Darwin's backers and opponents were often heated, but few were as dramatic as an incident that occurred in June 1860 at Oxford University in England. It was one of the most famous debates in the history of science. Darwin's leading opponents planned to destroy both his theory and his reputation. To make the attack, they chose a respected bishop, Samuel Wilberforce. Darwin was too ill to attend, so two of his friends and fellow scientists, Thomas Huxley and Joseph Hooker, stood in for him.

More than 700 people attended the debate. Most probably expected Wilberforce to demolish Darwin and the notion of evolution. Speaking first, the bishop tried to do exactly that. He asked whether anyone in the audience had ever seen an animal evolving. None had, of course, because the process requires thousands of years. He claimed that this proved that evolution did not exist. Wilberforce also asked if turnips might eventually evolve into humans. This was an attempt to mislead the audience. Darwin had never claimed that plants evolved into animals.

When Wilberforce had finished his attacks, Huxley addressed the crowd. He countered many of the bishop's arguments. Huxley also pointed out that Wilberforce did not seem to

Samuel Wilberforce, Lord Bishop of Winchester (1805–1873)

grasp the ideas he was condemning. Finally it was Hooker's turn to speak. He held the audience spellbound for more than two hours. Using logic and facts, he explained Darwin's main ideas one by one.

When the debate was over, it was Wilberforce's reputation, not Darwin's, that had been damaged. The initial battle between Darwin's supporters and opponents was over. His supporters had won.

Thomas Huxley passionately defended Darwin's theory of evolution at the Oxford University debate.

CHAPTER FIVE

Modern Views of Evolution

DARWIN'S COLLEAGUES had convincingly won the debate at Oxford in 1860. But the larger dispute over the merits of his theory of evolution did not end there. Nor did it end with his death in 1882. In the decades that followed, writers, politicians, religious leaders, and other critics kept up their attacks.

These efforts to discredit the theory of evolution were largely unsuccessful. The ideas in Darwin's book had permanently changed science. They had also reshaped the way science is taught in schools. By 1920 almost every college and high school in the United States taught evolution. The same was true across Europe. In addition, new evidence confirming the process of evolution continued to pour in. Several major scientific discoveries in the 1900s strengthened most of Darwin's arguments.

The introduction of evolution into biology classes was largely because of Darwin.

Should Schools Teach Only Evolution?

Although most scientists accept evolution as fact, some people do not. Many of them are religious people who accept the biblical explanation of life's origins. Many creationists feel it is misleading to teach only evolution in school. They want the biblical version of creation to be taught as well. Giving both versions, they say, provides students with a more balanced education.

Creationists have scored occasional successes. For example, in 1995, they persuaded the state school board in Alabama to place stickers on the biology textbooks stating that evolution is a "controversial theory" that only "some scientists" accept. It has since been rewritten but remains in place.

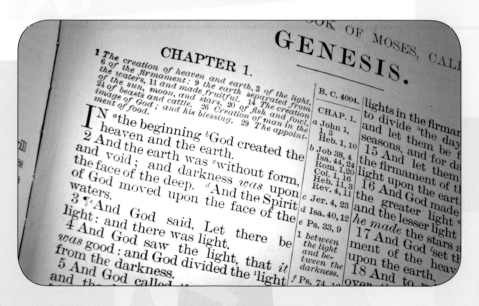

The book of Genesis in the Old Testament details the story of creation. It says God created Earth and all living things in six days.

GENETICS AND MUTATIONS

One reason Darwin's theory has been widely accepted by scientists is that it has repeatedly stood up to challenges. One important challenge came in the early 1900s, when the new science of genetics was emerging. Researchers had discovered that tiny structures called genes exist in the cells of living things. They determined that genes carry the genetic information—or blueprints—for making all living things.

At first some experts wondered whether an unknown factor in the genes might cause evolution. They suggested that Darwin's natural selection was not the driving force after all. Instead, large-scale mutations might be the answer. A mutation is a sudden, random change in one or more genes.

A team of botanists—scientists who study plants—experimented with genetically modified plants at a genetics laboratory.

Most mutations are tiny and have little effect on the physical makeup of an organism's offspring. But every now and then a larger mutation occurs. It can produce a more noticeable physical change. Some scientists thought these bigger mutations caused life to evolve over time.

This idea was contrary to Darwin's theory. He had insisted that evolution results from many small changes that occur gradually over time. Many scientists later concluded that Darwin had been right. As the science of genetics progressed, it became clear that larger mutations are almost always harmful. Beneficial changes come from smaller mutations that accumulate over time. For example, a small mutation might make an insect's color slightly darker. As a result, the insect blends better with the tree it lives in. Creatures that normally eat that insect would have a harder time finding it,

Several flowers developed from the stalk of a mutated dandelion.

so the insect would have a better chance of surviving. Several generations later, another small genetic change might give the insect another survival advantage, such as slightly longer legs. This would allow the insect to run a little faster and more easily escape from predators.

A beetle's body color allows it to hide against the bark of a tree, making the insect difficult for predators to see.

LATER DISCOVERIES

The evolutionary synthesis, which combined evolutionary theory and genetics, was further strengthened by later discoveries. Since the 1950s, scientists have come to understand the structure of DNA—the molecule in all living things that carries the genetic material. Studying DNA has taught researchers that various species are genetically related. This has provided evidence for the argument that each species has evolved from earlier ones.

Another important development in modern evolutionary theory concerns human origins. For a long time scientists tried to understand how the human brain had evolved. They hoped to explain how advanced intelligence came to be. Some saw an upward progression in evolution. In other words, there seemed to be a natural tendency for the brains of living creatures to become more complex over time. The result was the human brain.

Other researchers argued that there is no such natural tendency toward increasing brain complexity. They agreed

---

DID YOU KNOW?

The term *modern synthesis* in evolution first appeared in 1942. It was coined by the biologist Julian Huxley, a grandson of Charles Darwin's close friend and supporter Thomas Huxley.

---

with Darwin, who held that evolution is completely random. Darwin believed that evolution had clearly produced higher intelligence. But he thought it had happened by chance rather than through any kind of natural law. Studies of many human fossils found in the 1900s confirmed this. They showed that the development of bigger brains had not been a sure thing. Rather, higher intelligence developed through a series of "lucky accidents."

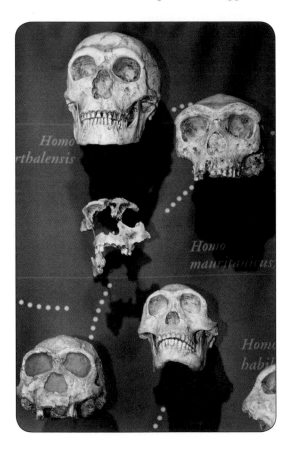

These and other discoveries in the past century have shown that evolution is real and that it continues today. They also show that the basic ideas of Darwin's explanation of evolution were correct. In the words of the world-famous American biologist Ernst Mayr, "The basic theory of evolution has been confirmed so completely that modern biologists consider evolution simply a fact."

The American Museum of Natural History in New York displayed a variety of skulls in honor of Charles Darwin.

controversial—tending to cause disagreement, disputes, and debates

DNA—deoxyribonucleic acid, the molecule in the cells of living things that contains the blueprints of life

evolutionary synthesis—combination of the theory of evolution and the science of genetics

extinction—elimination of an animal or plant species

fossil—hardened remains or impressions of dead plants and animals

genes—basic genetic units in DNA molecules

genetics—science of heredity, or how the blueprints of life pass from one generation to another

geologists—scientists who study rocks and Earth's structure

modification—in genetics, a change in physical form caused by changes in DNA

molecule—microscopic particle consisting of two or more atoms

mutation—in genetics, a random change in one or more genes

natural selection—process driving evolution by which random changes in offspring determine the fittest for survival

naturalist—in the 1800s, someone who studied plants and animals

transitional form—species that has some features of its ancestors and some of its descendants

▶ Charles Darwin was eager to join the crew of the *Beagle*, but his father, Robert Darwin, was against it. Charles' uncle, Josiah Wedgwood, heard about the dispute. He wrote to Robert Darwin and urged him to change his mind, which he did. The voyage, which might not have happened if not for Wedgwood, turned out to be crucial in the formation of Darwin's evolutionary ideas.

▶ Evidence shows that over time, land animals evolved from sea creatures. But the opposite is also true. For example, scientists believe that whales did not originate in the sea. They think whales evolved from early land creatures called pakicetids. These mammals existed more than 50 million years ago. They looked like dogs but had hoofed feet. Pakicetids spent part of their lives in the water. Their descendants adapted to living in the water by developing legless bodies. They still needed to breathe air into their lungs, though. That is why whales regularly swim to the surface for air.

▶ The process of evolution can be affected by another process—extinction. Many species have died out in the past. Occasionally a large natural disaster causes many species to become extinct. This is called mass extinction. When many species disappear suddenly, remaining species have fewer predators and fewer competitors for food and other resources. Such major changes in their environment can produce a rapid burst of evolution. This is what scientists think happened when a large asteroid struck Earth 65 million years ago. The impact wiped out the dinosaurs and many other species. Mammals—which were mouse-like creatures at that time—survived. They evolved into thousands of new and successful species, including humans.

Many scientists believe that the extinction of the dinosaurs occurred when an asteroid with a diameter of 6.25 miles (10 km) smashed into the Yucatan Peninsula in southeastern Mexico.

Further Reading

Jenkins, Steve. *Life on Earth: The Story of Evolution.* Boston: Houghton Mifflin, 2002.

Lawson, Kristan. *Darwin and Evolution for Kids: His Life and Ideas with 21 Activities.* Chicago: Chicago Review Press, 2003.

Nardo, Don. *The Importance of Charles Darwin.* San Diego: Lucent Books, 2005.

Sis, Peter. *The Tree of Life: Charles Darwin.* New York: Farrar, Straus, and Giroux, 2003.

Internet Sites

FactHound offers a safe, fun way to find Internet sites related to this book. All of the sites on FactHound have been researched by our staff. Here's all you do:
Visit *www.facthound.com*
Facthound will fetch the best sites for you!

On the Road

Down House, Home of Charles Darwin
Kent, England BR6 7JT
01689 859119

The Hall of Human Origins
American Museum of Natural History
Central Park West and 79th Street
New York, NY 10024-5192
212/769-5100

Explore all the Life Science books

Animal Cells: The Smallest Units of Life

DNA: The Master Molecule of Life

Food Webs: Interconnecting Food Chains

Genetics: A Living Blueprint

Human Body Systems: Maintaining the Body's Functions

Major Organs: Sustaining Life

Plant Cells: The Building Blocks of Plants

A complete list of Exploring Science titles is available on our Web site: *www.compasspointbooks.com*